GROUNDED
FORSAKEN & DESERTED AEROPLANES

GROUNDED
FORSAKEN & DESERTED AEROPLANES

GRAHAM ROBSON

Motorbooks International
Publishers & Wholesalers

This USA edition published in 1992 by Motorbooks International, Publishers & Wholesalers, PO Box 2, 729 Prospect Avenue, Osceola, WI 54020, USA.

© Graham Robson 1992
Published by Airlife Publishing Ltd., Shrewsbury, England, 1992.

Printed and bound in Singapore by Kyodo Printing Co (S'pore) Pte Ltd

The information in this book is true and complete to the best of our knowledge. All recommendations are made without any guarantee on the part of the author or publisher, who also disclaim any liability incurred in connection with the use of this data or specific details.

We recognize that some words, model names and designations, for example, mentioned herein are the property of the trademark holder. We use them for identification purposes only. This is not an official publication.

Library of Congress Cataloguing-in-Publication Data
ISBN 0-87938-665-7

Motorbooks International books are also available at discounts in bulk quantity for industrial or sales-promotional use. For details write to Special Sales Manager at the Publisher's address.

INTRODUCTION

'Whatever happened to . . .' and 'do you remember that old . . .' — expressions that could refer to those once common, though long forgotten, aircraft types often taken for granted by the more complacent photographer.

Few people give more than a passing thought to the eventual fate of the many different aircraft they have grown up with, as they were replaced or superseded by more modern versions, with the originals simply fading from memory. Many words and pictures appear covering the newest and latest types, both in the civilian and military fields, yet very little coverage is given to those whose flying career has now come to an end. This book is not intended as a guide of what to see, and where — there are other far more specialist titles available which chronicle such things. *Grounded*, as the title suggests, serves more as an illustrated cross section of those aircraft which have managed to hang on to some kind of existence long after their flying days have ended.

Mention of grounded aircraft immediately brings to mind the huge storage site at Davis Monthan Air Force Base, in the United States. The unique AMARC is a phenomenon of the vast resources of the US military machine, and its disposition process, and is almost certainly unrivalled anywhere. However, certain parts of the world, for various reasons, have become synonymous with particular aircraft types, Dan Air's long association with the Comet at Lasham and Perpignan's Europe Air Services with their love of the Vanguard being two good examples. In both cases the majority of all survivors of the breed gathered as a source of spares to help keep the lucky few in the air a little longer. With the recent replacement of the Phantom in the Air Defence role of the RAF by the Tornado, RAF Wattisham has become the collection point for all retired examples and their subsequent demise, while the ageing Canberra force presently being run down will meet a similar fate at RAF Wyton.

Throughout the world similar comparisons can be made; southern Florida's appetite for time expired piston types is well known, and the vast airliner storage sites in the south western USA have filled in recent years as their industry has changed and modernised its fleets. Certain foreign air forces have major aircraft collection and storage sites, such as Chateaudun in France or the Belgian Air Force's base at Koksijde, where the majority of the respective air forces' retired fleets have gathered for disposal. Their fate is more often than not in the hands of the local scrapman, either directly or after a time on the fire dump. Some types, fortunately, have managed to survive and begin a new lease of life, often in a different country. Notable examples are the ex-Spanish Air Force C-47s and CASA 352Ls or the ex-Belgian Air Force Pembroke fleet, which found their way onto the civilian market during the late 1970s.

Most of the aircraft shown in *Grounded* fall into four main categories: those withdrawn from use and awaiting a decision on their fate; those being readied for or in the process of being scrapped; fire practice and crash rescue training; and finally, a now very familiar role at many European and North American bases, that of Battle Damage Repair Training airframes. Others such as maintenance trainers or airfield decoy aircraft also appear, though to a lesser extent. Peter Blanchard and Aiden Curley both kindly helped in supplying some shots from their collections, which together with the author's work have made up the final selection of illustrations.

It should be borne in mind that a lot of the aircraft pictured in this book were not easily accessible for photography: areas such as fire dumps and aircraft scrapping areas on military bases are normally well away from any active ramps, often in a restricted part of the airfield, and close inspection with a camera can often be misinterpreted by someone inside the fence.

Opposite: The introduction of the GR.5 and GR.7 versions of the Harrier into front line service with the RAF has seen the fleet of earlier GR.3 models phased out during the late 1980s. Most aircraft were picked clean of parts at RAF St. Athan, South Wales before being passed out to bases for other duties. Here, ex-1 Squadron Harrier GR.3 XV740 lies in the long grass at RAF Abingdon in Oxfordshire in August 1989 for use with the BDR training unit.

Opposite: Republic F-105G Thunderchief 62-4428 last served with the Georgia Air National Guard before being retired to the MASDC (now AMARC), and an uncertain future. Wearing slightly unauthentic markings, as '63428' it serves as the Battle Damage Repair Training airframe at RAF Upper Heyford, Oxfordshire.

Below: A long term resident of Tucson airport, Fairchild C-82 Packet 44-23033 still shows signs of its former operator, the USAF's Military Air Transport Service, on its boom. So few good examples of this type remain, that the Tucson Packet must surely be a worthy candidate for preservation.

Opposite: Looking rather forlorn, Army Air Corps Scout AH.1 XP191 was photographed in July 1988 at the home of Army flying, Middle Wallop, England. Its flying days now over, it will eventually end up on the airfield's fire dump.

Below: Hunter F.6 XF526 last flew with 4FTS at RAF Valley in Wales, whose red and white training scheme it was seen wearing when photographed in March 1989. Fitted with the tail fin from a different Hunter, the picture shows it in the scrapping area of RAF St. Athan, South Wales, the last resting place for many retired aircraft over the years.

Below: Proudly wearing its 'Mig kill' marking on the splitter plate, F-4D 66-7661 sits on the maintenance ramp of the District of Columbia Air National Guard base at Andrews Air Force Base in May 1990. Last flown by the DC ANG, it has been retained for eventual display, although it shows no signs of this so far.

Opposite: Vulcan XH560 was one of the six examples converted to K.2 standard in June 1983, to augment the Victor tanker force, with the addition of three long range fuel tanks in the bomb bay and a refuelling hose and drogue unit fitted in the ECM bay of the tailcone, visible in the photo. The four Olympus engines have been removed and sit below the Vulcan on the fire dump at RAF Marham in March 1991, prior to the scrapman beginning his job.

Opposite: Douglas C-133B Cargomaster 90531 last flew with the 437th MAW before being replaced by the C-141A Starlifter. Withdrawn to the MASDC (now AMARC) in 1972, it was sold onto the civilian market as N2276V and flown to nearby Tucson airport, where it has remained parked ever since.

Below: Exotic T-28 Fennec HR-228, late of the Honduran Air Force, is seen parked with a few of its stablemates at Fort Lauderdale Executive Airport in Florida during October 1984, Abandoned since 1980 at the airport, their eventual destination was never confirmed, doubtless most succumbed to the local scrap dealer.

Below: Replaced in the refuelling role by a further batch of VC-10s and the Tristar tankers, the Victor K.2 fleet at RAF Marham in Norfolk is running down fast in 1991. XL512 sits withdrawn from use on the south side of the base in March 1991, ominously close to the fire dump.

Opposite: In its final years with the RAF the entire Lightning fleet was based at RAF Binbrook in Lincolnshire. With the introduction of the ADV Tornado into front line service, both the Lightnings and their base became redundant. The entire stock of remaining airframes was moved outside for eventual scrapping. In this photograph, T.5 XS457 with all useful parts missing and all markings overpainted awaits its turn in May 1988.

Opposite: A definite candidate for restoration, this valuable
Douglas A-26 Invader wearing civil registration N550 looks
slightly weatherbeaten but otherwise intact. Parked out at Opa
Locka airport near Miami, Florida since the early 1980s, it was
photographed in October 1984.

Below: Probably the last flyable Connie to come out of AMARC,
EC-121H presently resides in the yard of Desert Eagle Aviation,
Tucson, one of the many scrapyards around the perimeter of
Davis Monthan AFB. When photographed in October 1990 the
owners were hopeful of selling the Constellation in a flyable
condition, rather than letting it become scrap metal.

Below: During the last few years the importance of Aircraft Battle Damage has been recognised in the military, and consequently most USAFE bases were issued with redundant aircraft on which to practice. The 48th TFW at RAF Lakenheath received F-4C 37610 from the 171st FIS Michigan ANG on 16 July 1986, and is seen here not long after, wearing the scars from its new job.

Opposite: Showing signs of its previous operator, and evidently not long out of storage at AMARC, Douglas C-117D 99857, allocated the appropriate civil registration N99857, will no doubt soon end up one of the growing number of more contemporary 'warbirds' privately owned in the United States. Photographed at Opa Locka, Florida in October 1984.

Opposite: Bierget Aviation based at Chandler, Arizona operate a fleet of ex-military Douglas C-54 Skymasters as budworm sprayers and freighters. Having been received from the MASDC in February 1975, C-54Q 56528 has served as a source of spares for the fleet ever since, although was allocated registration N44915.

Below: Wearing the markings of all the resident Phantom units at George Air Force Base, California, and carrying the 'WW' tail code of the based 35th FW, F-4C 64-0910 now serves as a maintenance training airframe.

Opposite: One of eleven Nimrod airframes converted to AEW.3 standard in the early 1980s, envisaged as the replacement for the Shackleton in the Airborne Early Warning role, XZ286 lies in the Battle Damage Repair Flight pan at RAF Abingdon, Oxfordshire awaiting the scrapman's torch. The airframes of these Nimrods were considered too extensively modified for de-conversion back to Maritime Reconnaisance fit, and declared surplus.

Below: Seen outside the Base Fire Station at the home of the U.S. Air Force Flight Test Centre, Edwards AFB, Douglas A-3A Skywarrior 135434 seems doomed to eventual destruction. Photographed in October 1987, the aircraft has since been earmarked for possible restoration by the base museum.

Opposite: A sorry end to a magnificent aeroplane. Boeing KC-97L 22605 last served with the Wisconsin Air National Guard, before being retired to the MASDC at Davis Monthan AFB, Tucson, Arizona, in January 1978. It was sold four years later and is seen in one of the reclamation yards on the edge of the base in October 1982, undergoing parts recovery for other more fortunate examples of the type.

Below: Lightning F.2A XN734, now wearing British class B markings G27-239, was used for many years as a systems and maintenance trainer for the Royal Saudi Air Force at BAe Warton in England. Sold off after that country's Lightnings were withdrawn, it was resident at Cranfield, Bedfordshire in June 1988 acting as a spares source in the restoration project on a series T.5 Lightning.

Below: Even after their flying career has ended, some aircraft are still very useful in other ways. Employed as a 'decoy' on a mock airfield in the Otterburn military ranges in Northumberland, Sea Vixen FAW.2 XJ604, with some parts missing seems to have a good while left yet as a target for attacking aircraft.

Opposite: 'Old film stars never die . . .' A one-time star of the motion picture 'Hannover Street', B-25N Mitchell 44-30925 (NL9494Z) lies seemingly abandoned by its owners, 'Warbirds of the World', at Coventry airport in January 1991. Dismantled in several pieces, it will take a lot of hard work to get this beast flying again.

Opposite: Looking in a very poor way, and no doubt destined for worse, Pembroke C.52 83016/86 is used as a crash rescue training airframe at the Swedish Air Force Base of Satenas, and was photographed in August 1990. (Aiden Curley)

Below: With engines, outer wing panels and many other parts missing, ex-111 Squadron Phantom FG.1 XT872/BT bides its time on the flight line at RAF Wattisham, Suffolk in February 1991, prior to being moved to the base's fire dump for scrapping. A one-time Fleet Air Arm aeroplane, it was transferred to the Air Force after the demise of the Royal Navy's fixed wing aircraft carriers, and eventually retired in January 1990.

Below: Folland Gnat T.1 XM706 of 4FTS was allocated the maintenance serial 8572M when transferred to RAF Halton in England as an apprentices training aid. Unfortunately, the souvenir hunters struck when the Gnat was moved onto the fire dump of RAF Swinderby, Lincoln in March 1990, the serial having been neatly removed.

Opposite: Flight Systems Inc., a civilian flight test company based at Mojave, California operate a varied fleet of aircraft on numerous test programmes, both for the civilian market and on government contract. Its test days now over, this F-100D Super Sabre has had its registration overpainted and is now in open storage on Mojave's north side.

Opposite: With all traces of identification removed before leaving the MASDC, this brightly coloured Grumman US-2A Tracker keeps company with over forty similar types in the yard of Consolidated Aeronautics, Tucson. This Tracker will no doubt be acting as a source of spares for the many examples used in the fire bomber role in Canada, North America and France.

Below: Mimicking a Soviet fighter, complete with nose and tail markings, this one-time Belgian Air Force T-33 is actually serving a very useful purpose. FT-11 now resides on the electronic warfare range at RAF Spadeadam, in Cumbria, as a decoy aircraft.

Below: The classic Boeing KC-97 is still a valuable aeroplane long after its military career ended. Its massive lifting capability and power make it ideal for outsize cargo operations and fire bombing, though few airframes have been converted for the latter purpose. Hemet Valley Flying Services own this example N1365D, formerly 20895 of the Wisconsin ANG, which was photographed at their Stockton, California base in October 1990, whilst awaiting a decision on its future. Plans to have converted it for fire bombing were halted after the company obtained surplus military C-130 Hercules for the job.

Opposite: This front fuselage section from Boeing C-97G 17269 obviously has some value to someone, as the remainder of the airframe was reduced to scrap during 1977. Photographed in Allied Aircraft Sales' yard at Tucson, close to AMARC in October 1982, this Strat last flew with the base unit at Clark Air Base in the Philippines.

Opposite: Saab A.32 Lansen N4767R wore serial number 32120 during its military days flying with the Swedish Air Force, whose scheme it still wears. Since the early 1980s it has been a resident of Mojave, California, operated by Mach Two Flight Services Inc. but now seems withdrawn from use.

Below: Seen in the BDR training area at Middle Wallop AAC base, England in July 1988 is one of the Westland Lynx prototypes, in civilian Westland 606 guise. Painted in company demonstration colours, it has suffered badly at the hands of the repair training teams, looking too far gone for preservation.

Below: Wearing the distinctive colour scheme of the United States Coast Guard, Grumman HU-16E Albatross 2125 looks ready for the scrap man. This type, however, is proving popular for the 'warbird' collectors in the USA, and 2125 could very likely take flight again. Photographed in the yard of Dross Metals Inc, Tucson in October 1982.

Opposite: Its trial flying with the 6512 Test Squadron at Edwards Air Force Base now over, prototype Rockwell B-1A 40158 is seen in the process of being dismantled during October 1987, for a move to its new home. Set to become an instructional airframe at Hanscom AFB, Massachusetts, the Air Force museum would, perhaps, have been a more fitting destination for this particular B-1.

Opposite: The USAF base at Mildenhall, Suffolk had this pair of BDR airframes in April 1990. VC-140B Jetstar 24198, which last flew with the 58 MAS at Ramstein AB in Germany arrived in September 1987, to join the F-4C 40707, resident since July 1986. The Phantom has since been moved to nearby RAF Lakenheath to join similar types already there.

Below: The years between 1970 and 1974 saw the majority of the remaining Lockheed C-121 Constellations in active U.S. Navy Service retired. This NC-121K was operated by the Naval Research Laboratory at Patuxtent River NAS in Maryland until August 1974, when it was flown to the MASDC for storage. Released for sale in 1981, it moved the short distance to Allied Aircraft Sales' yard, where it was eventually scrapped.

Opposite: Not much remains of this Andover C.1 from which to identify it as XS594, the prototype of the 'tall tailed' Andover variant. Photographed in August 1988 after being cleared from the Otterburn ranges, where it had literally been shot to pieces during its time as a target 'decoy' aircraft since March 1984.

Below: With panels open and pieces missing, Canberra B.2 WJ603 is almost fighting for its continued existence. Last flown by 100 Squadron, it was delivered to RAF Wattisham in Suffolk in the early 1980s, and allocated maintenance serial 8664M for BDR use. With a surplus of Phantoms now available to fulfil this duty, the Canberra has recently been scrapped and removed.

Opposite: This Nimrod MR.2 seems unlikely to ever fly again. XV257 suffered a bad internal fire on take off from RAF St. Mawgan in Cornwall on 3 June 1984, and has been out of service ever since. Ferried to BAe Woodford for repairs, it has languished outside for the last two years minus various parts. With the proposed reduction in the Nimrod fleet, this particular example would seem a likely candidate for permanent grounding.

Below: Wearing fake Soviet Air Force markings, and masquerading as Mig fighters, these three Mystere IVs are part of the 'decoy' air force in place on the electronic warfare range at RAF Spadeadam in Cumbria. Photographed in August 1988, their non-destructive future looks assured for the time being.

Opposite: Former U.S. Navy F-8A Crusader 145385, latterly used by NASA for research and chase duties, rests in a slightly derelict condition in the storage compound of the base museum at Edwards AFB, in October 1987.

Below: Shackleton AEW.2 WL745 suffers an undignified end at the RAF Fire Fighting School at Catterick, North Yorkshire. This Shackleton, the prototype AEW.2 was one of twelve converted in 1971 as a 'stop gap' until the introduction of the Nimrod AEW variant. It was retired after the government defence cuts of 1981 reduced the Shackleton force by half.

Opposite: Of the eleven AEW Nimrods converted XV263 remains the most complete. Now used by the Aircraft Engineering Squadron as a ground trainer at RAF Finningley in Yorkshire, and allocated maintenance number 8967M, it arrived from storage at RAF Waddington, Lincoln in July 1987.

Below: Canberra B.2 8515M, the one-time WH869, was assigned to the Aircraft Salvage and Repair Unit at RAF Abingdon in Oxfordshire. The airframe was used to train crews in the recovery, salvage and transportation of downed aircraft. Photographed in August 1990, it has since been reduced to scrap.

Below: Former 60 Squadron Pembroke C.1 XF796 now a long way from home. Registered N2692U, the aircraft was photographed, seemingly abandoned at Hollister airport, California in October 1989.

Opposite: Now in the twilight of its career, the Victor K.2 force will soon be totally replaced by more VC-10 tankers. At the home of the Victor, RAF Marham in Norfolk, XL160 has been on the dump since June 1986 and is set to be joined by more in the near future.

Opposite: Held in open storage until needed by Flight Systems Inc. at Mojave, these former South African Air Force Sabres will be returned to flying status eventually. Filled with complex avionics, they will fly as pilotless 'drones' acting as live targets in weapons firing trials by the military. Here, Canadair built Sabres 350, 352, 363 and 371 await their call to duty.

Below: The 159th Fighter Interceptor Squadron of the Florida ANG, now an F-16 operator, previously flew the Convair F-102 Delta Dagger in the early 1970s. 70817 was retained by the squadron for use as a crash rescue trainer at their base at Jacksonville Airport, Florida. Photographed there in November 1980. (Peter Blanchard)

Opposite: Shackleton MR.3 WR974/K, allocated maintenance number 8117M, was previously in use for ground instruction training at No. 2 SoTT at RAF Cosford in England. Disposed of in early 1989, along with sistership WR982/J, both were being dismantled during April for the move to their new home in Surrey, to join a growing museum collection.

Below: Vintage Curtis C-46 44-77559 basks in the late afternoon Arizona sunshine, in October 1982. Held in storage for twenty years at MASDC, it was released by the Air Force in 1978 and has remained untouched ever since, even through various ownership changes over the years. (Peter Blanchard)

Below: After a lengthy test programme with the USAF, U.S. Navy and NASA the Hawker Siddeley P.1127 trials were abandoned in 1966. XV-6A Kestrel 64-18264, number 4 in the programme, was relegated to a life in the wilderness of the vast Edwards AFB ranges. Recovered in 1982, when it was photographed on the Edwards ramp it was refurbished and now resides in the United States Army Aviation Museum at Fort Rucker, Alabama. (Peter Blanchard)

Opposite: This unidentified Vought F7U Cutlass had been part of the scenery at Fort Lauderdale Executive Airport, Florida for a long time when photographed in November 1980. Not much else is known about this rare aircraft, though it had gone by October 1984, hopefully to a better home in some museum. (Peter Blanchard)

Opposite: 40160 was the third Rockwell B-1A built, and spent its flying career as a test aircraft at Edwards AFB, California. Photographed after retirement in October 1987, and wearing a non-standard camouflage scheme, its duties necessitated slight modifications to its spine. The B-1A now serves as a ground instructional trainer at Lowry AFB, Colorado.

Below: The TBM Avenger more than proved itself during World War II as a strong reliable aeroplane. Such qualities gave it a new lease of life in the 1960s as a fire bomber within North America. Superseded by more powerful, though not always more modern types in the 1970s, many TBMs were left abandoned until being acquired by collectors on the 'war bird' circuit. N9569Z, photographed at Mesa, Arizona in 1982 was last flown by locally based Globe Air, and still shows signs of its former U.S. Navy colours. (Peter Blanchard)

Below: Douglas C-133A Cargomaster N201AR, the former USAF 20001, has remained parked at Mojave airport for the last fifteen years, in company with similar type N136AR. Both still in very good condition, they are held as spares sources for airworthy example N199AB which operates with the appropriately named Cargomaster Corporation out of Anchorage, Alaska.

Opposite: Nord N.2501 Noratlas looks a little out of place in a garden behind the village petrol station in St. Peravy-la-Colombe, France in September 1987. Withdrawn from French Air Force service in 1976, the Noratlas was stored at the nearby base at Chateaudun before being dismantled in 1978 and sold.

Opposite: The busy RAF base at Wildenrath in northern Germany was home to a large fleet of BDR airframes in 1991. Here Lightning F.3 XN778 (foreground) and F.6 XR727 are parked inside a revetment on the western end of the base in May 1991.

Below: Since reunification in Germany the RAF Phantom squadrons at Wildenrath, which had manned the QRA 'Battle Flight' have been stood down, and will both have been disbanded by 1992. With impending base closure, the need for so many BDR airframes became unnecessary. Consequently, the resident 431 Maintenance Unit saw this as an opportunity for explosives and salvage training, all at once.

Opposite: A sad day for RAF Scampton in Lincolnshire was 14 November 1986, when the base's preserved Vulcan B.2 XH563 was unceremoniously cut up for scrap. Last operated by 27 Squadron, it was preserved wearing the unit markings of all Scampton's Vulcan Squadrons. The bulk of the airframe was reduced to scrap, but as the photograph shows, the nose section could someday end up being preserved.

Below: Parked close to the Lightnings at Wildenrath is the Phantom 'lair', with FGR.2 examples from 92 Squadron XV394/T and 19 Squadron XV478/B, as well as former 111 Squadron FG.1 XV569/BQ.

Below: The Breguet 765 Sahara would never have won any prizes for beauty, but was the original 'heavylifter'. Struck off charge from the French Air Force in 1969, 501/64-PE is seen outside the aero club buildings at Evreux in August 1983 in fairly good condition, apparently preserved.

Opposite: Nicknamed 'Dodo', after the extinct flightless bird is this aptly named Shackleton AEW procedure trainer at RAF Lossiemouth in Scotland. Actually the fuselage and inner wings from MR.2C WR967, grounded after a heavy landing, are now used in the training of Fighter Controllers in the RAF's AEW force. This April 1991 photograph shows the trainer in its last days of 'active' duty, the Shackleton force being withdrawn shortly afterwards and replaced by the E-3D Sentry two months later.

Opposite: Some Dassault Mystere IVs funded for the French Air Force by the Military Assistance Programme found their way to various USAFE bases during the late 1970s. RAF Lakenheath received no less than twelve examples, which were repainted in a tactical camouflage scheme and used as airfield decoys. The ravages of time, and attention by the resident BDR teams have taken their toll on the aircraft, as seen in September 1988.

Below: This photograph shows the demise of Phantom FGR.2s at Wildenrath in the summer of 1991.

Below: The USAF base at Alconbury has two F-4 Phantom training airframes parked out on the airfield. This ex-Air Force F-4C 63-7419 still wears its last unit's full markings, from the 182TFS Texas Air National Guard. Flown to Alconbury in summer 1986, its condition still seems very good, as this August 1991 photograph shows.

Opposite: Photographed in pieces on the dump at RAF Cottesmore in July 1991 is Jet Provost T.3 XM375. Wearing old 'style RAF' Training Command scheme, it had spent the last few years at RAF Halton as a training aid for engineering apprentices.

Opposite: Unusual tactical camouflage adorns this Pembroke C.1 WV701, parked in the BDR revetment area of RAF Wildenrath in Germany in May 1991. Last flown in the VIP role by based unit 60 Squadron, the camouflage pattern was an addition since being withdrawn from service in March 1987.

Below: This Fairchild Provider is described on its data block under the flightdeck window as a C-123T. The letter T denotes a proposed Turbo-prop conversion, to give the type a new lease of life. Unfortunately, work never began on the conversion programme, and it was dropped in the early 1980s, the Provider 64357 owned by the Thai Air Force has remained parked at the contractors, Hamilton Aviation of Tucson ever since.

Below: Mojave airport in California has been the last resting place for a lot of retired airliners over the years. Here, Lockheed Electra HP-579 last flown by COPA of Panama is slowly being dismantled in this October 1990 photograph, with the last mortal remains of an ex-Air Force Convair T-29 in the foreground.

Opposite: One of a number of non-destructive fire training airframes at RAF Manston is Argosy E.1 XN855, with its Rolls Royce Dart engines removed, the aircraft is otherwise complete, as shown in this September 1991 photograph.

Opposite: The radical and unique conversion of Comet 4 XW626 can still not hide the beautifully graceful lines of the type. At one time flown by BOAC as G-APDS on its worldwide route network, it became a military Comet in 1969, acquiring its hideous nose profile in 1977 when engaged in the abortive Nimrod AEW programme, testing the GEC Avionics radar system. Last flown in August 1981, it has been parked outside at RAE Bedford ever since, its condition deteriorating badly over the years. The uncertain future of the airfield and the poor condition of the airframe give a sad outlook for this unique Comet.
(photo courtesey of MoD Bedford)

Below: One of a number of Devon C.2s which have met their fate at the CTE Fire School at RAF Manston in Kent. VP971 is now the only example of the type still in one piece at the base, and was photographed in September 1991 in the non-destructive training area.

Opposite: Seen in very poor condition at Las Vegas McCarren International Airport in October 1990 is the unique Ahrens 404. Built by the Ahrens Aircraft Company at Oxnard, California in the early 1970s, it never got beyond the prototype stage, and the hope of series production was never reached. Abandoned in the hot Nevada sun, this 'one off' deserves a better fate.

Below: T & G Aviation of Chandler, Arizona maintain a sizeable fleet of Douglas DC-6 and DC-7s used in the aerial tanker role. The task of keeping these beasts flyable is helped by a good stock of spares provided by a few non-flying examples. DC-7B N4885C, originally delivered to Delta Airlines in 1957, has had her engines robbed for valuable parts but otherwise looks complete.

Below: One-time military VC-121B 46-0608 named 'Dewdrop', Lockheed L-749A Constellation N608AS looks abandoned at Ryan Field, Arizona in October 1990. Bought from the defunct Globe Air at Mesa in 1985, it was flown to Ryan Field to serve as a spares source for two similar types which have since been returned to flying condition. Despite its unkempt look, the value of this rare type should guarantee its continued existence and possibly even eventual restoration.

Opposite: The most well known operator of the De Havilland Comet, Dan Air also had the distinction of flying the last ever commercial Comet service in November 1980. Dan Air's engineering base at Lasham was the graveyard for most of their large fleet, with the final Comet at Lasham G-BDIV surviving until summer 1985. The photograph shows the ex-RAF Comet 4C, one of only a handful to wear the revised colour scheme of the time, being reduced to scrap in July of that year.

Opposite: Wearing 'Proud Appeal' titles on the cabin roof, this ex-United Airlines DC-8 series 21 N8022U was well beyond its best at Fort Lauderdale International and heading for eventual dismantling, when photographed in October 1984.

Below: The Milestones of Flight Museum at Fox Field, Lancaster, California received this B-25C Mitchell N3968C, the one-time 41-13251, and A-20G Havoc N34920/43-22197 seen in the background from the late Howard Hughes in 1971, who had used them as executive transports with his Hughes Aircraft Company. During the following twenty years they have remained untouched, not even being fully re-assembled after being trucked in.

Opposite: DHC-4 Caribou N9013M last flew with the U.S. Army as 62-4145 in support of the missile range on the island of Kwajalein, part of the Marshall Islands in the Pacific. Disposed of in January 1987, after being replaced by Shorts 330s, this Caribou now lives at Van Nuys airport near Burbank, California in company with three similar types, and looks to be used as the spares source keeping the others airworthy.

Below: The scrapping of this unmarked and unidentified Fokker F.27 was well advanced when photographed at Tucson in October 1991. With most useful parts removed, all that remains is the bare fuselage, wings and tail fin.

Opposite: Bought from British Airways after retirement in the early 1980s, this Super VC-10 has been in open storage at RAF Abingdon in Oxfordshire pending conversion to a tanker for the RAF. Its appearance belies the actual good condition, with a sealant covering to protect the airframe from the elements. G-ASGI, allocated ZD237, is one of eleven Super VC-10s obtained by the RAF, though not all are due to be converted, some will be cannibalised for spares.

Below: Metroliner N70A ends its days in the compound of Hamilton Aviation at Tucson airport in October 1991. Still wearing the colours of its last operator, it is kept as a spares ship for other Metroliner users.

Below: The solitary Convair 990 at Mojave still wears its Aerolineas Peruanas S.A. colour scheme, with whom it flew between 1965 and 1973 before being withdrawn from use and stored, initially at Tucson and later Mojave. Photographed in October 1990, time has been kind to the oldest Coronado still in existence.

Opposite: Kingman, Arizona became famous as the final resting place for thousands of surplus World II Two bombers in the late 1940s, at the end of hostilities. Almost forty years later, the bulk of the British Airways Boeing 707 fleet met a similar fate on the same site. Photographed in September 1981, G-ARWD had been leased to Air Mauritius before being retired and still wore their livery when it arrived at Kingman. The tail fins in the foreground give a hint to the eventual fate of this 707.

Opposite: Another Van Nuys resident, though not for long, was second prototype DHC Dash 7 C-GNCA. Its useful life over, this high time test aircraft was sold for scrap, the process being well advanced when photographed in October 1989.

Below: Handley Page Herald G-BEZB flew with Channel Express on freight charters until late 1987, when it was withdrawn from use at Bournemouth Hurn in England. Seen in June 1988, it has been used as a source of spares for the other Heralds in the fleet.

Opposite: Withdrawn from use with British Airways in summer 1981 Trident 1C G-ARPR was flown to Teesside airport on 16 September of that year, and transferred to the CAA Fire School. Part of a fleet of airliners used to train fire crews, the Trident was put to work and soon consumed by numerous 'torchings'.

Below: Built for KLM Royal Dutch Airlines as PH-TGG in 1953, this Convair 340 was withdrawn from use and stored at Opa Locka, Florida in 1984, after flying for Mexican operator Aerotur, as XA-LOU. It remained grounded until 1987 when it was sold to an airline in Bolivia.

Below: 'Mystery Jet'. This interesting type began life as a De Havilland Vampire trainer before conversion to executive jet. A privately funded programme by an American company to offer a low cost executive jet based on the Vampire was, sadly, unsuccessful. A few airframes were converted by enlarging the fuselage pod and adding cabin windows before the project failed. This unidentified example was photographed near Las Vegas Skyharbour airport in October 1990.

Opposite: Wearing the titles of a now defunct air cargo operator, to whom it was leased, Air Bridge Merchantman G-APEG was photographed at East Midlands Airport in open storage during March 1988. The ex-BEA Vanguard, converted to all-freight configuration as a Merchantman never flew again, and now resides on the far side of the airport as an inmate of the fire dump.

Opposite: Returned to Boeing ownership after flying in Peru as OB-R-902, Boeing 727 series 63 N32720 was used as the flying test bed for Boeing's 'Ultra High Bypass' engine. Wearing company colour scheme, it was photographed at Mojave, California in October 1990 and withdrawn from use at the end of the test programme.

Below: Former British Midland Airways Viscount 814 G-AYOX is seen withdrawn from use at Teesside airport in early 1985 with all titles painted out. Stored with four other examples, all in need of wing spar work, it eventually departed by road to Exeter as a spares source with British Air Ferries.

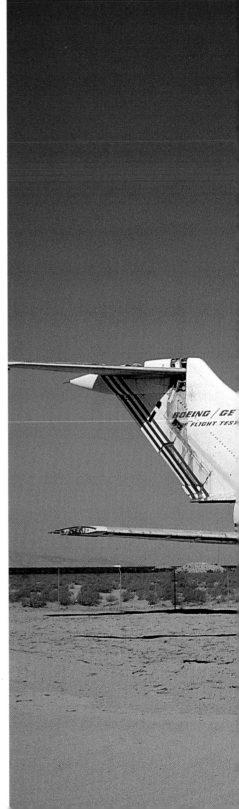

Below: Caribbean third-level airline Prinair were once the operators of the largest fleet of De Havilland Herons, the majority of which were converted in America by Riley Aircraft Company to become known locally as Turbo Skyliners. This conversion involved replacing the original Gypsy Queen engines with Avco Lycomings, giving much improved performance. After Prinair went out of business, their fleet of Riley Herons also went into demise, N578PR was photographed at Opa Locka, Florida in October 1984 looking very untidy.

Opposite: Last operated by Laker Airways as G-BFBZ, this Boeing 707-351B was flown to Lasham in April 1985 for storage after the airline's demise. Painted up to represent a BOAC aircraft for a part in a TV film, it was later robbed for spares, then left to the scrapmen. Looking in a sorry state in September 1988, it was eventually cut up and removed.

Opposite: Sold by Aviateca of Guatemala in January 1979, DC-6 TG-APA caused considerable embarrassment for the airline when it was seized four months later, still wearing full scheme, in southern Florida with an illegal cargo of narcotics. Impounded by the Broward County Sheriff's Department and stored at Fort Lauderdale International airport, it was photographed in October 1980, not long before being sold at auction for scrap.

Below: Parked out in the long grass outside the Naples Airlines maintenance base at Naples airport, Florida is Martin 404 N40403. Last operated by Piedmont Airlines, whose faded colours are still barely discernible, it was photographed in October 1984.

Below: Lee County Mosquito Control Division, based at Le High Acres airfield near Fort Myers in Florida operate an impressive fleet of vintage DC-3 Dakotas on spraying duties. This example, N101MX, was bought for spares after being involved in an accident which grounded the aircraft. It was photographed at Le High in October 1984.

Opposite and Overleaf: Noise regulations and modern equipment hastened the demise of the British Airways Trident fleet in the early 1980s. The series 3B soldiered on until the end of 1985 before finally bowing out. These photographs show the last moments of G-AWZE, retired in May 1983 and G-AYVF which flew its last service on February 1984, and were taken at the British Airways maintenance base at Heathrow in May 1984.

Opposite: The unmistakable profile of the ATL-98 Carvair. Few examples of this radical Douglas DC-4 conversion exist intact, illustrated is N55243 which last flew with Pacific Air Express out of Honolulu and was withdrawn after they ceased trading in March 1988. Flown to Naples Florida the following month, it was photographed there during October that year with its number 3 engine missing.

Opposite: One of a number of PV-2 Harpoon torpedo bombers converted for civilian use in the 1960s, N7251C sits alongside a similar type at Chandler Memorial Field, near Phoenix, Arizona in October 1990. The type may yet prove popular with the growing number of 'warbird' owners in the USA and waits patiently for the call.

Below: Air South, a Florida commuter airline last flew this Martin 404 N257S in 1981. Withdrawn from service, it was photographed at its Sarasota Bradenton base, in open storage during October 1984 in rather poor condition.

Below: 'The one that got away'. Douglas C-124C N3153F, in service with the USAF as 53-0044, was the last of its type to be retired to the MASDC, and one of the few to actually leave when it flew out to Las Vegas in the late 1970s. This smart looking Globemaster II is now parked in a compound close to the famous Las Vegas 'Strip', and ambitious plans to convert it into a casino seemed to have come to nothing when it was photographed in October 1987.

Opposite: Wearing the company titles of Dow Jones, following a short spell on lease to them from owners Florida Aircraft Leasing, Convair 440 N4814C had many parts missing when photographed in October 1988 at Fort Lauderdale International airport. Its poor condition not necessarily indicating the imminent death of this Convair, as the type is having a resurgence with many small freight operators.

Opposite: Photographed in a scrapyard close to Miami International airport in October 1980, DC-7BF HK-1300 last flew with Aeronorte Columbia before being retired in 1974. Reportedly scrapped in 1975, it lingered on as a forward fuselage and inner wings until 1982, when a runway extension at the airport forced the yard's closure, and the inevitable scrapping of the DC-7.

Below: Canadair CL-44J EI-BGO served Aer Turas well for almost ten years before being replaced by. . . another CL-44! Photographed in May 1989 alongside Dublin's north ramp, it was cannibalised for spares, then scrapped on site by a local contractor.

Below: Italian airline Aeropa flew this Boeing 707-321 N716HH on charter work in the 1970s, before it was bought by Aviation Traders of Stansted in England for spares reclamation. With all useful parts removed it was handed over to the CAA Fire School, then based at Stansted, and moved to their burning pans where it was photographed in July 1980. When the school moved to Teesside airport a few years later, the remaining airframes, including the 707 were sold to a scrap dealer and cut up.

Opposite: The last remains of Convair 990 N8356C sit forlornly in the scrapyard of Southwestern Alloys at Tucson in October 1987. Last flown by the travel club Denver Ports of Call, it was withdrawn in the mid-1980s, being sold for scrap soon afterwards.

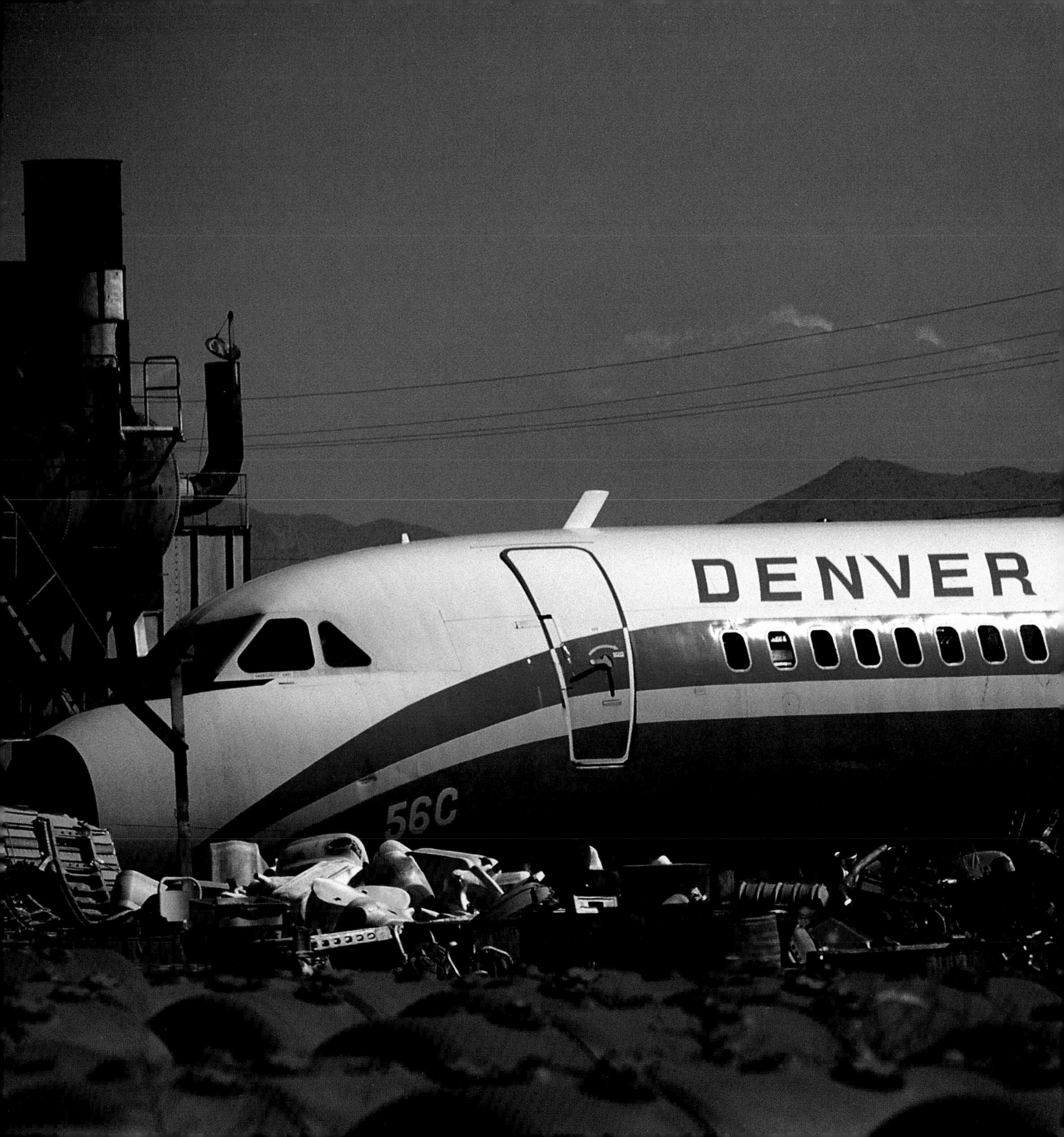
DENVER
56C

Opposite: N8108N was the twenty-fifth Boeing 727 to roll off the production line, spending its entire career flying for Eastern Airlines, themselves the first operator of the type. Retired to the Pinal Air Park, Marana in 1981, the photograph shows the situation seven years later, whilst awaiting the final axe.
(Peter Blanchard)

Below: American Transair retired this Boeing 707-123B N7515A in 1986, when it was flown to Kingman, Arizona. Its front fuselage has obviously found a good home as a training aid or museum piece, but the remainder of the airframe will be sold for its scrap value.

Below: Still wearing its old American Eagle colour scheme, Convair 580 N73165 is now used for spares by parcel carrier DHL keeping the rest of their Convair fleet flying. Photographed in May 1991, it has been a grounded Brussels Airport resident for three years.

Opposite: Grounded outside Aer Lingus' maintenance base at Dublin airport, Nigeria Airways Boeing 707-3F9C 5N-ANO was photographed in August 1991, Impounded and held for non-payment of maintenance fees, it has been parked minus engines for over twelve months.

Opposite: Aviation Traders at Stansted were responsible for the demise of many Boeing 707s during the 1970s and '80s. Bought, and scrapped for spares this ex-Pan American series 321C N884PA was typical of the many which ended their days at the Essex airport. It was photographed during dismantling in June 1986.

Below: Middle Eastern cargo airline New World Air Charter were once proud owners of a fleet of three Douglas DC-6s, operating from Dubai. One aircraft was abandoned there when the airline moved base to Larnaca, Cyprus, with another being lost in a crash in Oman in 1978. The company eventually folded leaving N19CA abandoned at Larnaca. Photographed in August 1985, the DC-6 was basically complete still wearing its long gone owner's titles.

Below: A dramatic end to Viscount 724 G-BDRC, last flown by Alidair it is now used as a training aid at RAF Manston's Fire School. In the aftermath of the M1 air crash, an airframe was needed to simulate a difficult access crash site, the Viscount proving ideal in this role.

Opposite: Flat tyres and fading paintwork appear to be all that is wrong with DC-6 N906MA when it was caught at Fort Lauderdale in October 1988. The one-time 'Mainliner Missouri' with United Airliners was grounded in 1981 after being bought by an aircraft trader and was eventually cut up for scrap.

Opposite: A sad end to the first DHC Dash 8, test aircraft C-GDNK was withdrawn from use in 1988 and ferried to Van Nuys, California where it was photographed in October 1990. The scrapmen had begun their work in taking the aircraft apart, with the nose section and flightdeck removed, hopefully saved for preservation.

Below: Nigerian charter operator Intercontinental Airways were the last user of this DC-8-51 5N-AVY before it was retired at Stansted and stored. Scrapping began at both ends of the fuselage, with only the centre section and wings remaining when photographed in September 1984.

Below: The distinctive cheat line of TWA is now well faded from Convair 880 N804AJ, after spending over ten years in open storage in the Mojave desert. The Convair took to the air for the last time in late 1989 when it was flown to Atlantic City, New Jersey for use by the FAA as a static test airframe.

Opposite: This Sikorsky UH-19 Chickasaw looks almost too far gone for any kind of restoration, but a company in Orlando, Florida have been collecting this old helicopter type over the years with definite plans for them. Under contract to the U.S. Army, Orlando Helicopters have begun a programme of rather radical conversions to transform the H-19 into Soviet 'Hind' Gunships, to be used as pilotless 'drones' at the White Sands Missile Range in New Mexico. This unidentified example awaits its turn on the 'production line' at Sanford, Florida in October 1988.